101

SURVIVAL TIPS

Also available from The Lyons Press

The Illustrated Guide to Wild Plants
The Illustrated Guide to Poisonous Snakes
The U.S. Army Combat Pistol Training Handbook
The U.S. Army Combat Skills Handbook
The U.S. Army Combat Stress Control Handbook
The U.S. Army Counterguerrilla Operations Handbook
The U.S. Army Counterintelligence Handbook
The U.S. Army Desert Operations Handbook
The U.S. Army First Aid Manual for Soldiers
The U.S. Army Fitness Training Handbook
The U.S. Army Intelligence and Interrogation Handbook
The U.S. Army Map Reading and Land Navigation Handbook
The U.S. Army Reconnaissance and Surveillance Handbook

101 Strategies for Self-Reliance in Any Environment
SURVIVAL TIPS

Department of the Army

The Lyons Press
Guilford, Connecticut

An imprint of The Globe Pequot Press

Contents

Introduction

I t takes much more than the knowledge and skills to build shelters, get food, make fires, and travel without the aid of standard navigational devices to live successfully through a survival situation. Some people with little or no survival training have managed to survive life-threatening circumstances. Some people with survival training have not used their skills and died. A key ingredient in any survival situation is the mental attitude of the individual involved. Having survival skills is important; having the will to survive is essential. Without a desire to survive, acquired skills serve little purpose and invaluable knowledge goes to waste.

There is a psychology to survival. The person in a survival environment faces many stresses that ultimately have an impact on his mind. Man has been able to survive many shifts in his environment throughout the centuries. His ability to adapt physically and mentally to a changing world kept him alive while other species around him gradually died off. The same survival mechanisms that kept our forefathers alive can help keep us alive as well. However, these survival mechanisms that can help us can also work against us if we don't understand and anticipate their presence.

Survival planning is nothing more than realizing something could happen that would put you in a survival situation and, with that in mind, taking steps to increase your chances of survival. Thus, survival means preparation.

Preparation means having survival items and knowing how to use them. People who live in snow regions, for example, prepare their vehicles for poor road conditions. They put snow tires on their cars, add extra weight in the back for traction, and they carry a shovel, salt, and blanket. Develop a survival plan that lets you beat the enemies of survival. This survival pattern must include food, water, shelter, first aid, and navigation placed in order of importance. For example, in a cold environment, you would first need a fire to get warm and then a shelter to protect you from the cold, wind, rain, or snow. After those needs were met, you could fashion traps or snares to get food, an improvised system to find your way back home, and first aid to maintain health. If you are injured, however, first aid is always the first priority no matter what climate you are in.

A true survivor is someone who can adjust his immediate physical needs as his environment changes. Follow the adage, "Hope for the best, prepare for the worst." It is much easier to adjust to pleasant surprises about one's unexpected good fortune than to be upset by one's unexpected harsh circumstances.

Chapter 1

Food Procurement

Although you can live several weeks without food, you need an adequate amount to stay healthy. Without food your mental and physical capabilities will deteriorate rapidly, and you will become weak. Food replenishes the substances that your body burns and provides energy. It provides vitamins, minerals, salts, and other elements essential to good health.

The two basic sources of food are plants and animals (including fish). In varying degrees both provide the calories, carbohydrates, fats, and proteins needed for normal daily body functions.

Calories are a measure of heat and potential energy. The average person needs 2,000 calories per day to function at a minimum level. An adequate amount of carbohydrates, fats, and proteins without an adequate caloric intake will lead to starvation and cannibalism of the body's own tissue for energy.

Tip 1. Eat whatever moves

You can, with relatively few exceptions, eat anything that crawls, swims, walks, or flies. The first obstacle is overcoming your natural aversion to a particular food source. Historically, people in starvation situations have resorted to eating everything imaginable for nourishment. A person who ignores an otherwise healthy food source due to a personal bias, or because he feels it is unappetizing, is risking his own survival. Although it may prove difficult at first, a survivor must eat what is available to maintain his health.

Tip 2. **Look for what's available**

To satisfy your immediate food needs, first seek the more abundant and more easily obtained wildlife, such as insects, crustaceans, mollusks, fish, and reptiles. These can satisfy your immediate hunger while you are preparing traps and snares for larger game.

Types of Birds	Frequent Nesting Places	Nesting Periods
Inland birds	Trees, woods, or fields	Spring and early summer in temperate and arctic regions; year round in the tropics
Cranes and herons	Mangrove swamps or high trees near water	Spring and early summer
Some species of owls	High trees	Late December through March
Ducks, geese, and swans	Tundra areas near ponds, rivers, or lakes	Spring and early summer in arctic regions
Some sea birds	Sandbars or low sand islands	Spring and early summer in temperate and arctic regions
Gulls, auks, murres, and cormorants	Steep rocky coasts	Spring and early summer in temperate and arctic regions

Knowing where and when birds nest makes catching them easier. Use this information to plan your attack.

Tip 3. Take birds from their roost

All species of birds are edible, although the flavor will vary considerably. You may skin fish-eating birds to improve their taste. As with any wild animal, you must understand birds' common habits to have a realistic chance of capturing them. You can take pigeons, as well as some other species, from their roost at night by hand. During the nesting season, some species will not leave the nest even when approached. Knowing where and when the birds nest makes catching them easier. Birds tend to have regular flyways going from the roost to a feeding area, to water, and so forth. Careful observation should reveal where these flyways are and indicate good areas for catching birds in nets stretched across some of the most promising areas for trapping or snaring.

Nesting birds present another food source—eggs. Remove all but two or three eggs from the clutch, marking the ones that you leave. The birds will continue to lay more eggs to fill the clutch. Continue removing the fresh eggs, leaving the ones you marked.

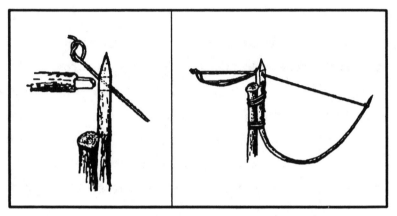

An Ojibwa bird pole is a snare used by Native Americans for centuries. To be effective, place it in a relatively open area away from tall trees. For best results, pick a spot near feeding areas, dusting areas, or watering holes.

Tip 4. Use an Ojibwa bird pole

Cut a pole 1.8 to 2.1 meters long and trim away all limbs and foliage. Sharpen the upper end to a point, then drill a small diameter hole 5 to 7.5 centimeters down from the top. Cut a small stick 10 to 15 centimeters long and shape one end so that it will almost fit into the hole. This is the perch. Plant the long pole in the ground with the pointed end up. Tie a small weight, about equal to the weight of the targeted species, to a length of cordage. Pass the free end of the cordage through the hole, and tie a slip noose that covers the perch. Tie a single overhand knot in the cordage and place the perch against the hole. Allow the cordage to slip through the hole until the overhand knot rests against the pole and the top of the perch. Spread the noose over the perch, ensuring it covers the perch and drapes over on both sides. As soon as the bird lands, the perch will fall, releasing the overhand knot and allowing the weight to drop. The noose will tighten around the bird's feet, capturing it.

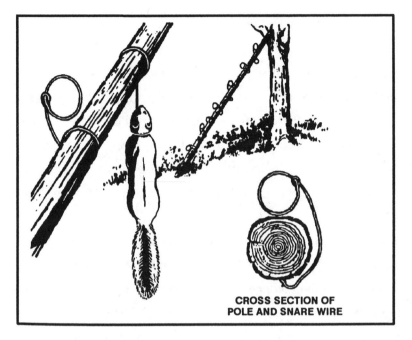

CROSS SECTION OF
POLE AND SNARE WIRE

Squirrels are tricky to catch. The squirrel pole simplifies this process by taking advantage of the squirrel's inherent curiosity.

Tip 5. Catch a squirrel

A squirrel pole is a long pole placed against a tree in an area showing a lot of squirrel activity. Place several wire nooses along the top and sides of the pole so that a squirrel trying to go up or down the pole will have to pass through one or more of them. Position the nooses (5 to 6 centimeters in diameter) about 2.5 centimeters off the pole. Place the top and bottom wire nooses 45 centimeters from the top and bottom of the pole to prevent the squirrel from getting its feet on a solid surface. If this happens, the squirrel will chew through the wire. Squirrels are naturally curious. After an initial period of caution, they will try to go up or down the pole and will get caught in a noose. The struggling animal will soon fall from the pole and strangle. Other squirrels will soon follow and, in this way, you can catch several squirrels. You can emplace multiple poles to increase the catch.

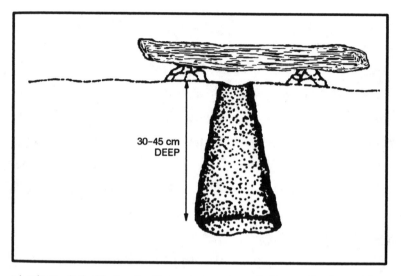

A bottle trap is the ideal method for capturing mice and other small rodents without killing them.

Tip 6. Dig a bottle trap for rodents

A bottle trap is a simple trap for mice and voles. Dig a hole 30 to 45 centimeters deep that is wider at the bottom than at the top. Make the top of the hole as small as possible. Place a piece of bark or wood over the hole with small stones under it to hold it up 2.5 to 5 centimeters off the ground. Mice or voles will hide under the cover to escape danger and fall into the hole. They cannot climb out because of the wall's backward slope. Use caution when checking this trap; it is an excellent hiding place for snakes.

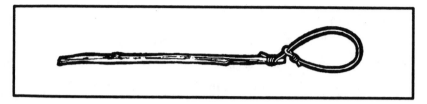

A noosing wand requires patience and perseverance. Simple to make, it is very effective for catching birds or small mammals.

Tip 7. Make a noosing wand

A "noosing wand" is useful for capturing roosting birds or small mammals. It requires a patient operator. This wand is more a weapon than a trap. It consists of a pole (as long as you can effectively handle) with a slip noose of wire or stiff cordage at the small end. To catch an animal, you slip the noose over the neck of a roosting bird and pull it tight. You can also place it over a den hole and hide in a nearby blind. When the animal emerges from the den, you jerk the pole to tighten the noose and thus capture the animal. Make sure to carry a stout club to kill the prey.

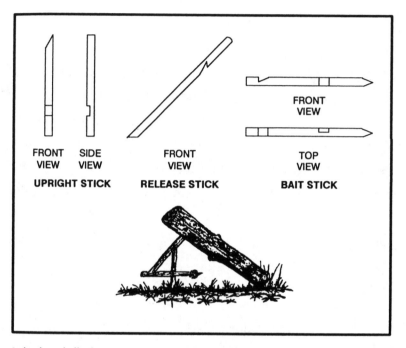

A simple and effective trap, a Figure 4 deadfall can be made to any size. A horizontal bait bar is balanced at right angles to an upright with a lock bar, which supports a rock or other heavy weight pivoting around the tip of the upright.

Tip 8. Assemble a Figure 4 deadfall

The Figure 4 is a trigger used to drop a weight onto a prey and crush it. The type of weight used may vary, but it should be heavy enough to kill or incapacitate the prey immediately. Construct the Figure 4 using three notched sticks. These notches hold the sticks together in a Figure 4 pattern when under tension. Practice making this trigger beforehand; it requires close tolerances and precise angles in its construction.

A Paiute deadfall is easier to set than a Figure 4. But as with all traps, use extreme caution when setting them. Otherwise you may face serious injury.

Tip 9. Build a Paiute deadfall

The Paiute deadfall is similar to the Figure 4 but uses a piece of cordage and a catch stick. It has the advantage of being easier to set than the Figure 4. Tie one end of a piece of cordage to the lower end of the diagonal stick. Tie the other end of the cordage to another stick about 5 centimeters long. This 5-centimeter stick is the catch stick. Bring the cord halfway around the vertical stick with the catch stick at a 90-degree angle. Place the bait stick with one end against the drop weight, or a peg driven into the ground, and the other against the catch stick. When a prey disturbs the bait stick, it falls free, releasing the catch stick. As the diagonal stick flies up, the weight falls, crushing the prey.

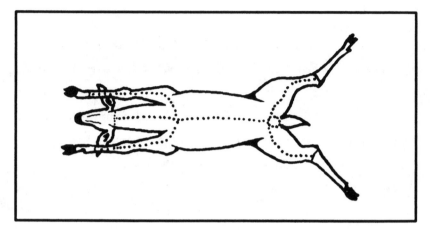

This simple diagram shows the cut lines necessary in skinning and butchering large game.

Tip 10. Skin and gut large game

Bleed the animal by cutting its throat. If possible, clean the carcass near a stream. Place the carcass belly up and split the hide from the throat to tail, cutting around all sexual organs. Remove the musk glands at points to avoid tainting the meat. When cutting the hide, insert the knife blade under the skin and turn the blade up so that only the hide gets cut. This will also prevent cutting hair and getting it on the meat.

Cut the gullet away from the diaphragm. Roll the entrails out of the body. Cut around the anus, then reach into the lower abdominal cavity, grasp the lower intestine, and pull to remove. Remove the urine bladder by pinching it off and cutting it below the fingers. If you spill urine on the meat, wash it to avoid tainting the meat. Save the heart and liver. Cut these open and inspect for signs of worms or other parasites. Also inspect the liver's color; it could indicate a diseased animal. The liver's surface should be smooth and wet and its color deep red or purple. If the liver appears diseased, discard it. However, a diseased liver does not indicate you cannot eat the muscle tissue.

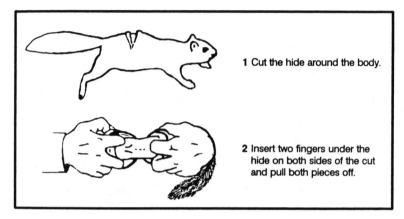

1 Cut the hide around the body.

2 Insert two fingers under the hide on both sides of the cut and pull both pieces off.

Skinning small game is much simpler process requiring fewer incisions than it does with larger game.

Tip 11. Skin and gut small game

For smaller mammals, cut the hide around the body and insert two fingers under the hide on both sides of the cut and pull both pieces off. Cut off the head and feet.

Remove the entrails from smaller game by splitting the body open and pulling them out with the fingers. Do not forget the chest cavity.

Tip 12. Prepare game for cooking

Cut larger game into manageable pieces. First, slice the muscle tissue connecting the front legs to the body. There are no bones or joints connecting the front legs to the body on four-legged animals. Cut the hindquarters off where they join the body. You must cut around a large bone at the top of the leg and cut to the ball and socket hip joint. Cut the ligaments around the joint and bend it back to separate it. Remove the large muscle (the tenderloin) that lie on either side of the spine.

Separate the ribs from the backbone. There is less work and less wear on your knife if you break the ribs first, then cut through the breaks.

Cook large pieces of meat over a spit or boil them. You can stew or boil smaller pieces, particularly those that remain attached to bone after the initial butchering, as soup or broth. You can cook body organs such as the heart, liver, pancreas, spleen, and kidneys using the same methods as for muscle meat. You can also cook and eat the brain. Cut the tongue out, skin it, boil it until tender, and eat it.

Tip 13. Preserve meat for future use

In addition to smoking (see page 25), you can preserve meat by using the following methods:

- Drying. To preserve meat by drying, cut it into 6-millimeter strips with the grain. Hang the meat strips in a sunny location with good air flow. Keep the strips out of the reach of animals and cover them to keep blowflies off. Allow the meat to dry thoroughly before eating. Properly dried meat will have a dry, crisp texture and will not feel cool to the touch.
- Freezing. In cold climates, you can freeze and keep meat indefinitely. Freezing is not a means of preparing meat. You must still cook it before eating.
- Brine and salt. You can preserve meat by soaking it thoroughly in a saltwater solution. The solution must cover the meat. You can also use salt by itself. Wash off the salt before cooking.

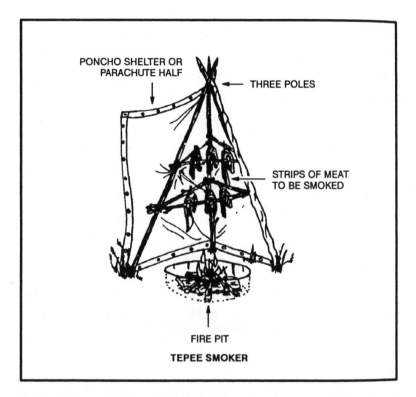

PONCHO SHELTER OR
PARACHUTE HALF

THREE POLES

STRIPS OF MEAT
TO BE SMOKED

FIRE PIT

TEPEE SMOKER

Meat smoked overnight using this method will keep for at least one week. Two days of smoking will preserve meat for two to four weeks.

Tip 14. Smoke your own meat

To smoke meat, prepare an enclosure around a fire. Two ponchos snapped together or a tarp will work. The fire does not need to be big or hot. The intent is to produce smoke, not heat. Do not use resinous wood in the fire because its smoke will ruin the meat. Use hardwoods to produce good smoke. The wood should be somewhat green. If it is too dry, soak it. Cut the meat into thin slices, no more than 6 centimeters thick, and drape them over a framework. Make sure none of the meat touches another piece. Keep the poncho enclosure around the meat to hold the smoke and keep a close watch on the fire. Do not let the fire get too hot. Meat smoked overnight in this manner will last about 1 week. Two days of continuous smoking will preserve the meat for 2 to 4 weeks. Properly smoked meat will look like a dark, curled, brittle stick and you can eat it without further cooking.

Tip 15. Prepare fish for cooking

Prepare a fish for eating as soon as possible after catching it. Cut out the gills and large blood vessels that lie near the spine. Gut any fish that is more than 10 centimeters long. Scale or skin the fish.

You can impale a whole fish on a stick and cook it over an open fire. However, boiling the fish with the skin on is the best way to get the most food value. The fats and oils are under the skin and, by boiling, you can save the juices for broth. You can use any of the methods used to cook plant food to cook fish. Pack fish into a ball of clay and bury it in the coals of a fire until the clay hardens. Break open the clay ball to get to the cooked fish. Fish is done when the meat flakes off. If you plan to keep the fish for later, smoke or fry it. To prepare fish for smoking, cut off the head and remove the backbone.

Tip 16. Avoid spoiled fish

Do not eat fish that appears spoiled. Cooking does not ensure that spoiled fish will be edible. Signs of spoilage are:

- Sunken eyes.
- Peculiar odor.
- Suspicious color. (Gills should be red to pink. Scales should be a pronounced shade of gray, not faded.)
- Dents stay in the fish's flesh after pressing it with your thumb.
- Slimy, rather than moist or wet body.
- Sharp or peppery taste.

Eating spoiled or rotten fish may cause diarrhea, nausea, cramps, vomiting, itching, paralysis, or a metallic taste in the mouth. These symptoms appear suddenly, one to six hours after eating. Induce vomiting if symptoms appear.

Tip 17. Don't discount worms

Worms (*Annelidea*) are an excellent protein source. Dig for them in damp humus soil or watch for them on the ground after a rain. After capturing them, drop them into clean, potable water for a few minutes. The worms will naturally purge or wash themselves out, after which you can eat them raw.

Chapter 2

Water Procurement

Your body loses water through normal

body processes (such as perspiration and digestion). During average daily exertion when the atmospheric temperature is 68 degrees Fahrenheit, the average adult loses and therefore requires 2 to 3 liters of water daily. Other factors, such as heat exposure, cold exposure, intense activity, high altitude, burns, or illness, can cause your body to lose more water. You must replace this water if you want to remain healthy.

Tip 18. Prevent dehydration

Of all the physical problems encountered in a survival situation, the loss of water is the most preventable. The following are basic guidelines for the prevention of dehydration:

- Always drink water when eating. Water is used and consumed as a part of the digestion process, which can lead to dehydration.
- Acclimatize. The body performs more efficiently in extreme conditions when acclimatized.
- Conserve sweat. Limit sweat-producing activities but drink water.
- Ration water. Until you find a suitable source, ration your water. A daily intake of 500 cubic centimeters (0.5 liter) of a sugar-water mixture (2 teaspoons per liter) will suffice to prevent severe dehydration for at least a week, provided you keep water losses to a minimum by limiting activity and heat gain or loss.

Tip 19. Consume the right amount

In any situation where food intake is low, drink 6 to 8 liters of water per day. In an extreme climate, especially an arid one, the average person can lose 2.5 to 3.5 liters of water per hour. In this type of climate, you should drink 14 to 30 liters of water per day.

With the loss of water there is also a loss of electrolytes (body salts). The average diet can usually keep up with these losses but in an extreme situation or illness, additional sources need to be provided. A mixture of 0.25 teaspoon of salt to 1 liter of water will provide a concentration that the body tissues can readily absorb.

Tip 20. Avoid certain fluids

Do not drink any of the following as a substitute for water:

- *Alcoholic beverages.* These liquids dehydrate the body and cloud judgment.
- *Urine.* It contains harmful body wastes and 2 percent salt.
- *Blood.* It is salty and considered a food; therefore, it requires additional body fluids to digest. It may also transmit disease.
- *Seawater.* It is about 4 percent salt. It takes about 2 liters of body fluids to rid the body of waste from 1 liter of seawater. Therefore, by drinking seawater you deplete your body's water supply, which can cause death.

Tip 21. Don't drink nonpotable water

By drinking nonpotable water you may contract diseases or swallow organisms that can harm you. Examples of such diseases or organisms are:

- *Dysentery*. Symptoms include severe, prolonged diarrhea with bloody stools, fever, and weakness.
- *Cholera and typhoid*. You may be susceptible to these diseases regardless of inoculations.
- *Flukes*. Stagnant, polluted water—especially in tropical areas— often contains blood flukes. If you swallow flukes, they will bore into the bloodstream, live as parasites, and cause disease.

Tip 22. Use snow and ice

Melt snow and ice and then purify. Do not eat snow or ice without melting first! Eating snow and ice can reduce body temperature and will lead to more dehydration. Remember that snow and ice are no purer than the water from which they come. Sea ice that is gray in color or opaque is salty. Do not use it without desalting it. Sea ice that is crystalline with a bluish cast has little salt in it.

Tip 23. Collect water from cacti

Cut off the top of a barrel cactus and mash or squeeze the pulp. Note that without a machete, cutting into a cactus is difficult and takes time since you must get past the long, strong spines and cut through the tough rind. Do not eat the pulp in the cactus but rather place the pulp in your mouth, suck out the juice, and discard the pulp.

Tip 24. Gather water on the beach

Dig a hole deep enough to allow water to seep in. Then obtain rocks, build a fire, and heat the rocks. Drop the hot rocks in the water and hold a cloth over the hole to absorb steam. Wring the water from the cloth. An alternate method if a container or bark pot is available is to first fill the container with seawater, then build a fire and boil the water to produce steam. This steam can be collected in a cloth, which is then wrung to produce potable water.

Tip 25. **Always purify water first**

Purify water by:

- Using water purification tablets. (Follow the directions provided.)

- Placing 5 drops of 2 percent tincture of iodine in a canteen full of clear water. If the canteen is full of cloudy or cold water, use 10 drops. (Let the canteen of water stand for 30 minutes before drinking.)

- Boiling water for 1 minute at sea level, adding 1 minute for each additional 300 meters above sea level, or boil for 10 minutes no matter where you are.

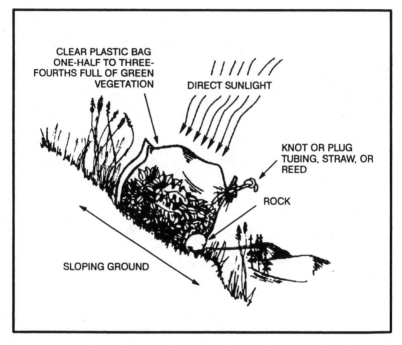

CLEAR PLASTIC BAG ONE-HALF TO THREE-FOURTHS FULL OF GREEN VEGETATION

DIRECT SUNLIGHT

KNOT OR PLUG TUBING, STRAW, OR REED

ROCK

SLOPING GROUND

You can use stills to gather water in various parts of the world. An aboveground water still uses solar energy to create condensation.

Tip 26. Construct an aboveground still

To make an aboveground still, you need a sunny slope on which to place the still, a clear plastic bag, green leafy vegetation, and a small rock.

- Fill the bag with air by turning the opening into the breeze or by "scooping" air into the bag.
- Fill the plastic bag half to three-fourths full of green leafy vegetation. Do not use poisonous vegetation. It will provide poisonous liquid. Be sure to remove all hard sticks or sharp spines that might puncture the bag.
- Place a small rock or similar item in the bag.
- Close the bag and tie the mouth securely as close to the end of the bag as possible to keep the maximum amount of air space.
- Place the bag, mouth downhill slightly higher than the low point in the bag, on a slope in full sunlight.
- Settle the bag in place so that the rock works itself into the low point in the bag.

To get the condensed water from the still, loosen the tie around the bag's mouth and tip the bag so that the water collected around the rock will drain out.

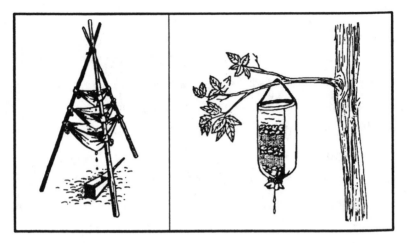

Rainwater collected in clean containers or in plants is usually safe for drinking. To be absolutely sure, one of these filtering systems should be used to improve the taste.

Tip 27. Improvise a water filter

If the water you find is muddy, stagnant, and foul smelling, you can clear the water:

- By placing it in a container and letting it stand for 12 hours.
- By pouring it through a filtering system.

These procedures only clear the water and make it more palatable. You will have to purify it.

To make a filtering system, place several centimeters of layers of filtering material such as sand, crushed rock, charcoal, or cloth in bamboo, a hollow log, or an article of clothing (see figure on opposite page). Remove the odor from water by adding charcoal from your fire. Let the water stand for 45 minutes before drinking it.

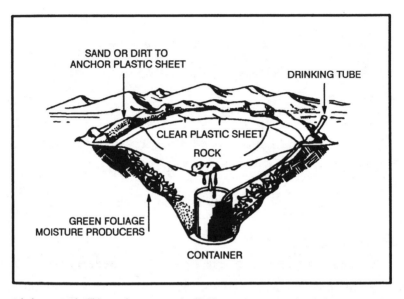

A belowground still is another means of collecting water. Because it is below ground, the water temperature remains somewhat cool.

Tip 28. Construct a belowground still.

To make a belowground still, you need a digging tool, a container, a clear plastic sheet, a drinking tube, and a rock.

Select a site where you believe the soil will contain moisture (such as a dry stream bed or a low spot where rainwater has collected). The soil at this site should be easy to dig, and sunlight must hit the site most of the day.

To construct the still:

- Dig a bowl-shaped hole about 1 meter across and 60 centimeters deep.
- Dig a sump in the center of the hole. The sump's depth and perimeter will depend on the size of the container that you have to place in it. The bottom of the sump should allow the container to stand upright.
- Anchor the tubing to the container's bottom by forming a loose overhand knot in the tubing.
- Place the container upright in the sump.
- Extend the unanchored end of the tubing up, over, and beyond the lip of the hole.

- Place the plastic sheet over the hole, covering its edges with soil to hold it in place.
- Place a rock in the center of the plastic sheet.
- Lower the plastic sheet into the hole until it is about 40 centimeters below ground level. It now forms an inverted cone with the rock at its apex. Make sure that the cone's apex is directly over your container. Also make sure the plastic cone does not touch the sides of the hole because the earth will absorb the condensed water.
- Put more soil on the edges of the plastic to hold it securely in place and to prevent the loss of moisture.
- Plug the tube when not in use so that the moisture will not evaporate.

You can drink the water without disturbing the still by using the tube as a straw.

Chapter 3

Shelter Basics

A shelter can protect you from the sun, insects, wind, rain, snow, and hot or cold temperatures. It can give you a feeling of well-being and a place to sleep.

In some areas, your need for shelter may take precedence over your need for food and possibly even your need for water. For example, prolonged exposure to cold can cause excessive fatigue and weakness. An exhausted person may develop a "passive" outlook, thereby losing the will to survive.

The most common error in making a shelter is to make it too large. A shelter must be large enough to protect you. It must also be small enough to contain your body heat, especially in cold climates.

Tip 29. Determine your shelter needs

Your environment and the equipment you carry with you will determine the type of shelter you can build. You can build shelters in wooded areas, open country, and barren areas. Wooded areas usually provide the best location, while barren areas have only snow as building material. Wooded areas provide timber for shelter construction, wood for fire, concealment from observation, and protection from the wind.

Tip 30. Select a shelter site

When you are in a survival situation and realize that shelter is a high priority, start looking for shelter as soon as possible. As you do so, remember what you will need at the site. Two requisites are:

- It must contain material to make the type of shelter you need.
- It must be large enough and level enough for you to lie down.

You must also remember the problems that could arise in your environment. For instance:

- Avoid flash flood areas in foothills.
- Avoid avalanche or rockslide areas in mountainous terrain.
- Avoid sites near bodies of water below the high water mark.

In some areas, the season of the year has a strong bearing on the site you select. Ideal sites for a shelter differ in winter and summer. During winter months you will want a site that will protect you from the cold and wind, but will have a source of fuel and water. During the summer months in the same area you will want a source of water, but you will want the site to be almost insect free.

Tip 31. Scout out natural shelters

Do not overlook natural formations that provide shelter. Examples are caves, rocky crevices, clumps of bushes, small depressions, large rocks on leeward sides of hills, large trees with low-hanging limbs, and fallen trees with thick branches. However, when selecting a natural formation:

- Stay away from low ground such as ravines, narrow valleys, or creek beds. Low areas collect the heavy cold air at night and are therefore colder than the surrounding high ground. Thick, brushy, low ground also harbors more insects.
- Check for poisonous snakes, ticks, mites, scorpions, and stinging ants.
- Look for loose rocks, dead limbs, coconuts, or other natural growth that could fall on your shelter.

A poncho tent uses an overhanging branch for support. It provides protection on two sides and is easily concealed.

Tip 32. Use a poncho to make a tent

This tent provides a low silhouette. It also protects you from the elements on two sides. It has, however, less usable space and observation area than a lean-to. To make this tent, you need a poncho, two 1.5- to 2.5-meter ropes, six sharpened sticks about 30 centimeters long, and two trees 2 to 3 meters apart. To make the tent:

- Tie off the hood of the poncho. Pull the drawstring tight, roll the hood longways, fold it into thirds, and tie it off.
- Tie a 1.5- to 2.5-meter rope to the center grommet on each side of the poncho.
- Tie the other ends of these ropes at about knee height to two trees 2 to 3 meters apart and stretch the poncho tight.
- Draw one side of the poncho tight and secure it to the ground pushing sharpened sticks through the grommets.
- Follow the same procedure on the other side.

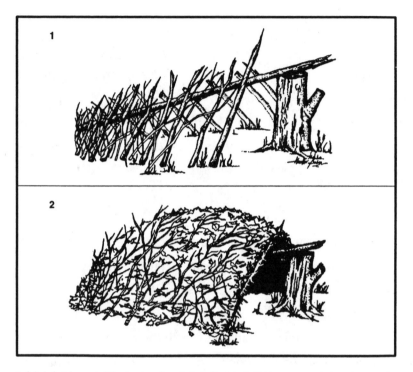

A debris hut is one of the best and easiest shelters to build in any wooded environment.

Tip 33. Make the classic debris hut

To make a debris hut:

- Construct a tripod with two short stakes and a long ridgepole or by placing one end of the ridgepole on top of a sturdy base.

- Secure the ridgepole (pole running the length of the shelter) using the tripod method or by anchoring it to a tree at waist height.

- Prop large sticks along both sides of the ridgepole to create a wedge-shaped ribbing effect. Ensure the ribbing is wide enough to accommodate your body and steep enough to shed moisture.

- Place finer sticks and brush crosswise on the ribbing. These form a latticework that will keep an insulating material (such as leaves) from falling through the ribbing onto the sleeping area.

- Add light, dry, soft debris over the ribbing until the insulating material is at least 1 meter thick—the thicker the better.

- Place a 30-centimeter layer of insulating material inside the shelter.

- At the entrance, pile insulating material that you can drag to you once inside the shelter to close the entrance.

- Add shingling material or branches on top of the debris layer to prevent the insulating material from blowing away in a storm.

A tree-pit snow shelter is ideal when you need to stay warm and well-hidden.

Tip 34. Dig a tree-pit shelter

If you are in a cold, snow-covered area where evergreen trees grow and you have a digging tool, you can make a tree-pit shelter. To make this shelter:

- Find a tree with bushy branches that provides overhead cover.
- Dig out the snow around the tree trunk until you reach the depth and diameter you desire, or until you reach the ground.
- Pack the snow around the top and the inside of the hole to provide support.
- Find and cut other evergreen boughs. Place them over the top of the pit to give you additional overhead cover. Place evergreen boughs in the bottom of the pit for insulation.

A beach shade shelter provides protection from the sun and heat, and it requires no special man-made materials to assemble.

Tip 35. Construct a beach shelter

This shelter protects you from the sun, wind, rain, and heat. It is easy to make using natural materials.

To make this shelter:

- Find and collect driftwood or other natural material to use as support beams and as a digging tool.
- Select a site that is above the high water mark.
- Scrape or dig out a trench running north to south so that it receives the least amount of sunlight. Make the trench long and wide enough for you to lie down comfortable.
- Mound soil on three sides of the trench. The higher the mound, the more space inside the shelter.
- Lay support beams (driftwood or other natural material) that spans the trench on top of the mound to form the framework for a roof.
- Enlarge the shelter's entrance by digging out more sand in front of it.
- Use natural materials such as grass or leaves to form a bed inside the shelter.

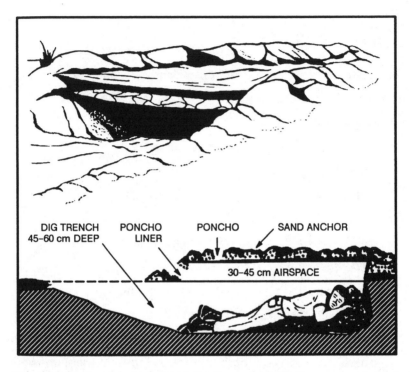

DIG TRENCH
45–60 cm DEEP

PONCHO
LINER

PONCHO

SAND ANCHOR

30–45 cm AIRSPACE

Make this belowground desert shelter when you are worried about overexposure in a hot and arid environment.

Tip 36. Build a desert shelter

A belowground shelter can reduce the midday heat as much as 30 to 40 degrees F. Building it, however, requires more time and effort than for other shelters. Since your physical effort will make you sweat more and increase dehydration, construct it before the heat of the day.

To make this shelter:

- Find a low spot or depression between dunes or rocks. If necessary, dig a trench 45 to 60 centimeters deep and long and wide enough for you to lie in comfortably.
- Pile the sand you take from the trench, dig out more sand so you can get in and out of your shelter easily.
- Cover the trench with your material.
- Secure the material in place using sand, rocks, or other weights.

If you have extra material, you can further decrease the midday temperature in the trench by securing the material 30 to 45 centimeters above the other cover. This layering of the material will reduce the inside temperature 20 to 40 degrees F.

The swamp bed is the perfect shelter to keep you dry in any area where there is standing water or wet ground.

Tip 37. Make a swamp bed

In a marsh or swamp, or any area with standing water or continually wet ground, the swamp bed keeps you out of the water. When selecting such a site, consider the weather, wind, tides, and available materials.

To make a swamp bed:

- Look for four trees clustered in a rectangle, or cut four poles (bamboo is ideal) and drive them firmly into the ground so they form a rectangle. They should be far enough apart and strong enough to support your height and weight, including equipment.
- Cut two poles that span the width of the rectangle. They, too, must be strong enough to support your weight.
- Secure these two poles to the trees (or poles). Be sure they are high enough above the ground or water to allow for tides and high water.
- Cut additional poles that span the rectangle's length. Lay them across the two side poles, and secure them.
- Cover the top of the bed frame with broad leaves or grass to form a soft sleeping surface.
- Build a fire pad by laying clay, silt, or mud on one corner of the swamp bed and allow it to dry.

Chapter 4

Making and Using Fire

In a survival situation, the ability to start a fire can make the difference between living and dying. Fire can fulfill many needs. It can provide warmth and comfort. It not only cooks and preserves food, it also provides warmth in the form of heated food that saves calories our body normally uses to produce body heat. You can use fire to purify water, sterilize bandages, signal for rescue, and provide protection from animals. It can be a psychological boost by providing peace of mind and companionship. You can also use fire to produce tools and weapons.

Fire can cause problems as well. It can cause forest fires or destroy essential equipment. Fire can also cause burns and carbon monoxide poisoning when used in shelters.

Remember to always weigh your need for fire against the problems that can spring from it.

Tip 38. Choose the right material

You need three types of materials to build a fire—tinder, kindling, and fuel.

Tinder is dry material, such as fine wood shavings, straw, dead grass and evergreen needles, that ignites with little heat. The tinder must be absolutely dry to be sure just a spark will ignite it. If you only have a device that generates sparks, charred cloth will be almost essential. It holds a spark for long periods, allowing you to put tinder on the hot area to generate a small flame. You can make charred cloth by heating cotton cloth until it turns black, but does not burn. Once it is black, you must keep it in an airtight container to keep it dry. Prepare this cloth well in advance of any survival situation. Add it to your individual kit.

Kindling is readily combustible material, such as small twigs, heavy cardboard, or split wood, that you add to the burning tinder. Again, this material should be absolutely dry to ensure rapid burning. Kindling increases the fire's temperature so that it will ignite less combustible material.

Fuel is less combustible material, such as coal, tree trunks and large branches, that burns slowly and steadily once ignited.

**STRAIGHT
FIRE
WALL**

**L-SHAPED
FIRE
WALL**

Fire walls will help direct or reflect heat where you want it. They also protect fires from burning out.

Tip 39. Select the right site

Before building a fire consider:

- The area (terrain and climate) in which you are operating.
- The materials and tools available.
- Time: how much time do you have?
- Need: why do you need a fire?

Look for a dry spot that:

- Is protected from the wind.
- Is suitably placed in relation to your shelter (if any).
- Will concentrate the heat in the direction you desire.
- Has a supply of wood or other fuel available.

If you are in a wooded or brush-covered area, clear the brush and scrape the surface soil from the spot you have selected. Clear a circle at least 1 meter in diameter so there is little chance of the fire spreading.

If time allows, construct a fire wall using logs or rocks. This wall will help to reflect or direct the heat where you want it. It will also reduce flying sparks and cut down on the amount of wind blowing into the fire. However, you will need enough wind to keep the fire burning.

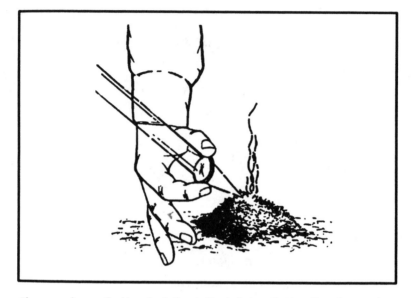

The convex lens method is a classic fire-starting technique that is well-worth mastering.

Tip 40. Light a fire using a lens

Before you start, always light your fire from the upwind side. Make sure to lay your tinder, kindling, and fuel so that your fire will burn as long as you need it.

Use the convex lens method only on bright, sunny days. The lens can come from binoculars, cameras, telescopic sights, or magnifying glasses. Angle the lens to concentrate the sun's rays on the tinder. Hold the lens over the same spot until the tinder begins to smolder. Gently blow or fan the tinder into flame, and apply it to the fire lay.

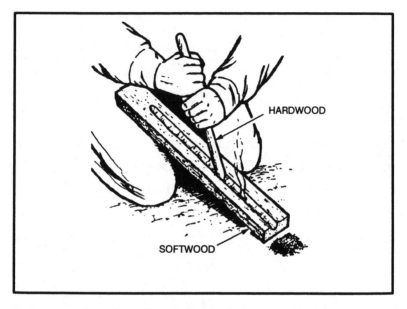

The fire-plow method relies on the use of hard and soft woods, a bit of elbow grease, and a little patience.

Tip 41. Use the fire-plow method

The fire-plow is a friction method of ignition. You rub a hardwood shaft against a softer wood base. To use this method, cut a straight groove in the base and plow the blunt tip of the shaft up and down the groove. The plowing action of the shaft pushes out small particles of wood fibers. Then, as you apply more pressure on each stroke, the friction ignites the wood particles.

TEPEE

A tepee fire is the best to use when you have wet wood.

Tip 42. Build a tepee fire

There are several methods for laying a fire, each of which has advantages. The situation you find yourself in will determine which fire to use.

To make this fire, arrange the tinder and a few sticks of kindling in the shape of a teepee or cone. Light the center. As the tepee burns, the outside logs will fall inward, feeding the fire. This type of fire burns well even with wet wood.

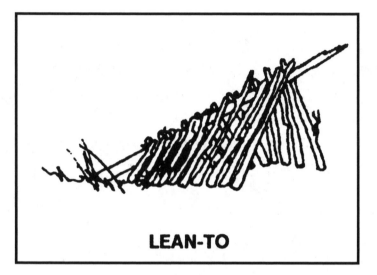

LEAN-TO

A lean-to fire relies on air circulation provided by its open structure.

Tip 43. Make a lean-to fire

To lay this fire, push a green stick into the ground at a 30-degree angle. Point the end of the stick in the direction of the wind. Place some tinder deep under this lean-to stick. Lean pieces of kindling against the lean-to stick. Light the tinder. As the kindling catches fire from the tinder, add more kindling.

PYRAMID

A pyramid fire requires no attention during the night.

Tip 44. Construct a pyramid fire

To lay this fire, place two small logs or branches parallel on the ground. Place a solid layer of small logs across the parallel logs. Add three or four more layers of logs or branches, each layer smaller than and at a right angle to the layer below it. Make a starter fire on top of the pyramid. As the starter fire burns, it will ignite the logs below it. This gives you a fire that burns downward, requiring no attention during the night.

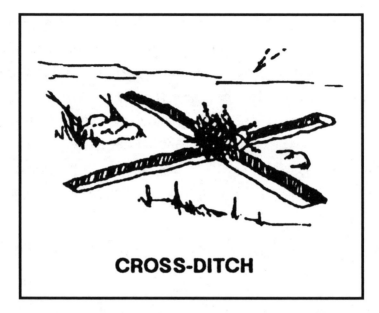

CROSS-DITCH

The cross-ditch method uses a ditch to provide the necessary draft for the fire.

Tip 45. **Assemble a cross-ditch fire**

To use this method scratch a cross about 30 centimeters in size in the ground. Dig the cross 7.5 centimeters deep. Put a large wad of tinder in the middle of the cross. Build a kindling pyramid above the tinder. The shallow ditch allows air to sweep under the tinder to provide a draft.

Build this base for a fire in snow-covered areas using green, wrist-sized logs.

Tip 46. Choose the right fire for snow

If you are in a snow-covered area, use green logs to make a dry base for your fire. Trees with wrist-sized trunks are easily broken in extreme cold. Cut or break several green logs and lay them side by side on top of the snow. Add one or two more layers. Lay the top layer of logs opposite those below it.

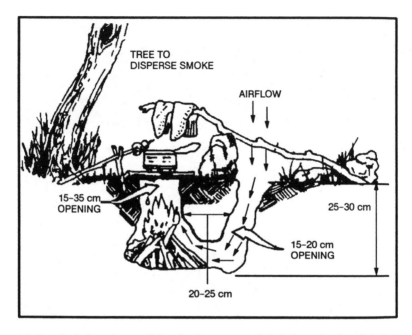

A Dakota fire hole makes an efficient fire that uses very little fuel. Another benefit is that it is also inconspicuous.

Tip 47. Make a Dakota fire hole

In some situations, you may find that an underground fireplace will best meet your needs. It conceals the fire and serves well for cooking food. To make an underground fireplace or Dakota fire hole:

- Dig a hole in the ground.
- On the upwind side of this hole, poke or dig a large connecting hole for ventilation.
- Build your fire in the hole as illustrated on the opposite page.

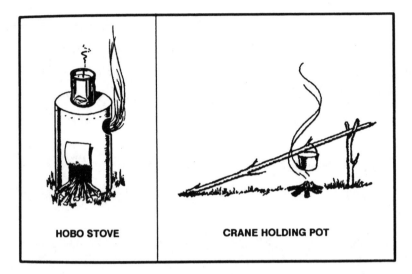

HOBO STOVE   **CRANE HOLDING POT**

The best fire for cooking is small in size and has hot coals and a place to hang or stand a pot.

Tip 48. Build a fire for cooking

In general, a small fire and some type of stove is the best combination for cooking purposes. A hobo stove is particularly suitable to the arctic. It is easy to make out of a tin can, and it conserves fuel. A bed of hot coals provides the best cooking heat. Coals from a crisscross fire will settle uniformly. Make this type of fire by crisscrossing the firewood. A simple crane propped on a forked stick will hold a cooking container over a fire.

Chapter 5

Basic Health and First Aid

Even under the most ideal circum- stances, nature is quite formidable. In a survival situation, a person will have to contend with the stressors of weather, terrain, and the variety of creatures inhabiting the area. Heat, cold, rain, winds, mountains, swamps, deserts, insects, and dangerous animals are just a few of the challenges awaiting the person working to survive. Depending on how a person handles the stress of his environment, his surroundings can be either a source of protection or food or can be a cause of extreme discomfort leading to injury, illness, or death.

Tip 49. Maintain good hygiene

In any situation, cleanliness is an important factor in preventing infection and disease. It becomes even more important in a survival situation. Poor hygiene can reduce your chances of survival.

A daily shower with hot water and soap is ideal, but you can stay clean without this luxury. Use a cloth and soapy water to wash yourself. Pay special attention to the feet, armpits, crotch, hands, and hair as these are prime areas for infestation and infection. If water is scarce, take an "air" bath. Remove as much of your clothing as practical and expose your body to the sun and air for at least 1 hour. Be careful not to sunburn.

Tip 50. **Keep your hands clean**

Germs on your hands can infect food and wounds. Wash your hands after handling any material that is likely to carry germs, after visiting the latrine, after caring for the sick, and before handling any food, food utensils, or drinking water. Keep your fingernails closely trimmed and clean, and keep your fingers out of your mouth.

Tip 51. Keep your clothing clean

Keep your clothing and bedding as clean as possible to reduce the chance of skin infection as well as to decrease the danger of parasitic infestation. Clean your outer clothing whenever it becomes soiled. Wear clean underclothing and socks each day. If water is scarce, "air" clean your clothing by shaking, airing, and sunning it for 2 hours. If you are using a sleeping bag, turn it inside out after each use, fluff it, and air dry it.

Tip 52. Keep your teeth clean

Thoroughly clean your mouth and teeth with a toothbrush at least once a day. If you don't have a toothbrush, make a chewing stick. Find a twig about 20 centimeters long and 1 centimeter wide. Chew one end of the stick to separate the fibers. Now brush your teeth thoroughly. Another way is to wrap a clean strip of cloth around your fingers and rub your teeth with it to wipe away food particles. You can also brush your teeth with small amounts of sand, baking soda, salt, or soap. Then rinse your mouth with water, salt water, or willow bark tea. Also, flossing your teeth with string or fiber helps oral hygiene.

Tip 53. Prevent blisters

Blisters are a common problem caused by friction. They may appear on such areas as the toes, heels, or the palm of the hand. Unless treated promptly and correctly, they may become infected. Prevention is the best solution to avoid blisters and subsequent infection. For example, ensure your boots are prepared properly for a good fit, whenever possible always keep feet clean and dry; and wear clean socks that also fit properly. Gloves should be worn whenever extensive manual work is done.

Keep blisters clean. Care should be taken to keep the feet as clean as possible at all times. Use soap and water for cleansing. Painful blisters or signs of infection, such as redness, throbbing, drainage, and so forth, are reasons for seeking medical treatment.

Tip 54. Treat blisters

If you get a small blister, do not open it. An intact blister is safe from infection. Apply a padding material around the blister to relieve pressure and reduce friction. If the blister bursts, treat it as an open wound. Clean and dress it daily and pad around it. Leave large blisters intact. To avoid having the blister burst or tear under pressure and cause a painful and open sore, do the following:

- Obtain a sewing-type needle and a clean or sterilized thread.
- Run the needle and thread through the blister after cleaning it.
- Detach the needle and leave both ends of the thread hanging out of the blister. The thread will absorb the liquid inside. This reduces the size of the hole and ensures that the hole does not close up.
- Pad around the blister.

Tip 55. Recover from a sprain

The accidental overstretching of a tendon or ligament causes sprains. The signs and symptoms are pain, swelling, tenderness, and discoloration (black and blue).

When treating sprains, think RICE:

R – Rest injured area

I – Ice for 24 hours, then heat after that.

C – Compression-wrapping and/or splinting to help stabilize. If possible, leave the boot on a sprained ankle unless circulation is compromised.

E – Elevation of the affected area.

Tip 56. Avoid CO₂ poisoning

Never fall asleep without turning out your stove or lamp. Carbon monoxide poisoning can result from a fire burning in an unventilated shelter. Carbon monoxide (CO_2) is a great danger. It is colorless and odorless. Any time you have an open flame, it may generate carbon monoxide. Always check your ventilation. Even in a ventilated shelter, incomplete combustion can cause carbon monoxide poisoning. Usually, there are no symptoms. Unconsciousness and death can occur without warning. Sometimes, however, pressure at the temples, burning of the eyes, headache, pounding pulse, drowsiness, or nausea may occur. The one characteristic, visible sign of carbon monoxide poisoning is a cherry red coloring in the tissues of the lips, mouth, and inside of the eyelids. Get into fresh air at once if you have any of these symptoms.

WIND SPEED	TEMPERATURE (°F)																	
Calm	40	35	30	25	20	15	10	5	0	−5	−10	−15	−20	−25	−30	−35	−40	−45
5 mph	36	31	25	19	13	7	1	−5	−11	−16	−22	−28	−34	−40	−46	−52	−57	−63
10 mph	34	27	21	15	9	3	−4	−10	−16	−22	−28	−35	−41	−47	−53	−59	−66	−72
15 mph	32	25	19	13	6	0	−7	−13	−19	−26	−32	−39	−45	−51	−58	−64	−71	−77
20 mph	30	24	17	11	4	−2	−9	−15	−22	−29	−35	−42	−48	−55	−61	−68	−74	−81
25 mph	29	23	16	9	3	−4	−11	−17	−24	−31	−37	−44	−51	−58	−64	−71	−78	−84
30 mph	28	22	15	8	1	−5	−12	−19	−26	−33	−39	−46	−53	−60	−67	−73	−80	−87
35 mph	28	21	14	7	0	−7	−14	−21	−27	−34	−41	−48	−55	−62	−69	−76	−82	−89
40 mph	27	20	13	6	−1	−8	−15	−22	−29	−36	−43	−50	−57	−64	−71	−78	−84	−91
45 mph	26	19	12	5	−2	−9	−16	−23	−30	−37	−44	−51	−58	−65	−72	−79	−86	−93
50 mph	26	19	12	4	−3	−10	−17	−24	−31	−38	−45	−52	−60	−67	−74	−81	−88	−95
55 mph	25	18	11	4	−3	−11	−18	−25	−32	−39	−46	−54	−61	−68	−75	−82	−89	−97
60 mph	25	17	10	3	−4	−11	−19	−26	−33	−40	−48	−55	−62	−69	−76	−84	−91	−98

To determine windchill, find the ambient air temperature on the top line of this chart, then read down the column to the line that corresponds with the current wind speed. Example: When the air temperature is 10° F and the wind speed is 20 mph, the rate of heat loss is equivalent to -9° F under calm conditions.

Tip 57. Protect against windchill

Windchill increases the hazards in cold regions. Windchill is the effect of moving air on exposed flesh. For instance, with a 27.8-kph (15-knot) wind and a temperature of -10 degrees C, the equivalent windchill temperature is -23 degrees C.

Remember, even when there is no wind, you will create the equivalent wind by skiing, running, or snowshoeing.

Clothing for cold weather should protect, insulate, and ventilate. Protect yourself by covering as large an area of the body as possible. Insulation will occur by trapping air which has been warmed by the body and holding it near the skin. Ventilate by allowing a two-way exchange of air through the various layers of clothing. Clothing should leave your body slightly cool rather than hot. It should also be loose enough to allow movement. Clothing soaked with perspiration should be removed if reasonably possible, and feet should be kept dry.

Do	Don't
• Periodically check for frostbite. • Rewarm light frostbite. • Keep injured areas from refreezing.	• Rub injury with snow. • Drink alcoholic beverages. • Smoke. • Try to thaw out a deep frostbite injury if you are away from definitive medical care.

There are several dos and don'ts to be aware of when it comes to treating frostbite.

Tip 58. Don't take frostbite lightly

This injury is a result of frozen tissues. Light frostbite involves only the skin that takes on a dull whitish pallor. Deep frostbite extends to a depth below the skin. The tissues become solid and immovable. Your feet, hands, and exposed facial areas are particularly vulnerable to frostbite.

A loss of feeling in your hands and feet is a sign of frostbite. If you have lost feeling for only a short time, the frostbite is probably light. Otherwise, assume the frostbite is deep. To rewarm a light frostbite, use your hands or mittens to warm your face and ears. Place your hands under your armpits. Place your feet next to your companion's stomach. A deep frostbite injury, if thawed and refrozen, will cause more damage than a nonmedically trained person can handle.

Tip 59. Prevent severe hypothermia

Hypothermia is the lowering of the body temperature at a rate faster than the body can produce heat. Causes of hypothermia may be general exposure or the sudden soaking of the body from falling into a pond, lake, or river, or through ice.

One of the quickest ways to get heat to the inner core is to give warm water enemas. Another method is to wrap the person in a warmed sleeping bag with another person who is already warm; both should be naked. However, a word of caution here, as the individual placed in the sleeping bag with the hypothermic person could also become a hypothermia victim if left in the bag too long.

If the person is conscious, give him hot, sweetened fluids. One of the best sources of calories is honey or dextrose; if unavailable, use sugar, cocoa, or a similar soluble sweetener. Never force an unconscious person to drink as this may cause choking.

Tip 60. Don't rewarm too quickly

There are two dangers in treating hypothermia—rewarming too rapidly and "after drop." Rewarming too rapidly can cause the victim to have circulatory problems, resulting in heart failure. After drop is the sharp body core temperature drop that occurs when taking the victim from warm water. Its probable cause is the return of previously stagnant limb blood to the core (inner torso) area as recirculation occurs. Concentrating on warming the core area and stimulating peripheral circulation will lessen the effects of after drop. Immersing the torso in a warm water bath, if possible, is the best treatment.

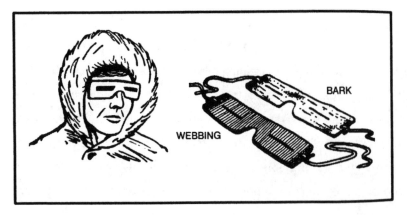

Sunglasses can be made out of a variety of the simplest materials. They are especially important in preventing snow blindness.

Tip 61. Prevent snow blindness

The reflection of the sun's ultraviolet rays off a snow-covered area causes snow blindness. The symptoms of this condition are a sensation of grit in the eyes, pain in and over the eyes that increase with eyeball movement, red and teary eyes, and a headache that intensifies with continued exposure to light. Prolonged exposure to these rays can result in permanent eye damage. To treat snow blindness, bandage your eyes until the symptoms disappear.

You can prevent snow blindness by wearing sunglasses. If you don't have sunglasses, improvise. Cut slits in a piece of cardboard, thin wood, tree bark, or other available material. Putting soot under your eyes will help reduce shine and glare.

Tip 62. Learn to recognize heat injuries and their symptoms

The following are common types of heat injuries and their symptoms:

- Heat cramps—muscle cramps of the abdomen, legs, or arms.
- Heat exhaustion—headache, excessive sweating, dizziness, nausea, clammy skin.
- Heat stroke—hot, dry skin, cessation of sweating, rapid pulse, mental confusion, unconsciousness.

To treat heat cramps, stop all activity, get in the shade, and drink water. To treat heat exhaustion, lie down in the shade, 45 centimeters off the ground, and have someone loosen your clothing and sprinkle you with water. Drink small amounts of water every 3 minutes. Stay quiet and rest. Heat stroke is sometimes accompanied by unconsciousness and is best left treated by a medical professional.

Chapter 6

Dangerous Animals and Plants

Animals rarely are as threatening to the survivor as the rest of the environment. Smaller animals actually present more of a threat to the survivor than large animals. To compensate for their size, nature has given many small animals weapons such as fangs and stingers to defend themselves. Each year more victims die from bites by relatively small venomous snakes than by large dangerous animals. Even more victims die from allergic reactions to bee stings.

Likewise, poisoning from dangerous plants ranges from mild irritation to death. Successful plant identification will help you avoid sustaining injuries from these plants. There is no one rule to aid in identifying poisonous plants. You must make an effort to learn as much about them as possible.

Tip 63. Remove the "sting" from a bee

If stung by a bee, immediately remove the stinger and venom sac, if attached, by scraping with a fingernail or a knife blade. Do not squeeze or grasp the stinger or venom sac, as squeezing will force more venom into the wound. Wash the sting site thoroughly with soap and water to lessen the chance of a secondary infection.

Tip 64. Handle a tick the correct way

If you find ticks attached to your body, cover them with a substance, such as Vaseline, heavy oil, or tree sap that will cut off their air supply. Without air, the tick releases its hold, and you can remove it. Take care to remove the whole tick. Use tweezers if you have them. Grasp the tick where the mouth parts are attached to the skin. Do not squeeze the tick's body. Wash your hands after touching the tick. Clean the tick wound daily until healed.

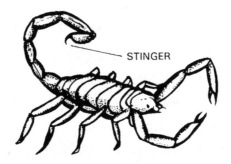

Scorpions are found in deserts, jungles, and forests of tropical, subtropical, and warm temperate areas of the world. Typically brown or black in moist areas, they may be yellow or light green in the desert.

Tip 65. Recognize scorpion bites

Scorpions are all poisonous to a greater or lesser degree. There are two different reactions, depending on the species:

- Severe local reaction only, with pain and swelling around the area of the sting. Possible prickly sensation around the mouth and a thick-feeling tongue.
- Severe systemic reaction, with little or no visible local reaction. Local pain may be present. Systemic reaction includes respiratory difficulties, thick-feeling tongue, body spasms, drooling, gastric distention, double vision, blindness, involuntary rapid movement of the eyeballs, involuntary urination and defecation, and heart failure. Death is rare, occurring mainly in children and adults with high blood pressure or illnesses.

The black widow spider is identified by a red hourglass on its abdomen. Only the female bites and carries the neurotoxic venom.

Tip 66. Treat stings or bites

Wash the area of the scorpion sting or black widow spider bite. Apply ice or freeze pack, if available. Apply baking soda, calamine lotion, or meat tenderizer to bite or sting site to relieve pain and itching. If site of bite or sting is on the face, neck (possible airway problems), or genital area, or if local reaction seems severe, or if the sting is by a dangerous type of scorpion found in the Southwest desert, keep the victim as quiet as possible and seek immediate medical aid.

Tip 67. Leave snakes alone

There are no infallible rules for expedient identification of poisonous snakes in the field, because the guidelines all require close observation or manipulation of the snake's body. The best strategy is to leave all snakes alone. When traveling in snake country, walk carefully and watch where you step. Step onto logs rather than over them before looking and moving on.

Tip 68. **Treat snakebite**

If you determine that a poisonous snake bit an individual, take the following steps:

- Reassure the victim and keep him still.
- Set up for shock and force fluids.
- Remove watches, rings, bracelets, or other constricting items.
- Clean the bite area.
- Maintain an airway (especially if bitten near the face or neck) and be prepared to administer mouth-to-mouth resuscitation or CPR.
- Use a constricting band between the wound and the heart.
- Immobilize the site.
- Remove the poison as soon as possible by using a mechanical suction device or by squeezing.

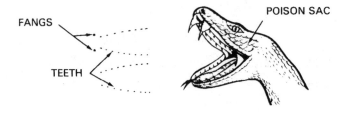

FANGS

TEETH

POISON SAC

A poisonous snake and the bite marks it leaves behind have easily recognizable characteristics that include fang puncture wounds.

Tip 69. Know the snake that bit you

Before your start treating a snakebite, determine whether the snake was poisonous or nonpoisonous. Bites from a nonpoisonous snake will show rows of teeth. Bites from a poisonous snake may have rows of teeth showing, but will have one or more distinctive puncture marks caused by fang penetration. Symptoms of a poisonous bite may be spontaneous bleeding from the nose and anus, blood in the urine, pain at the site of the bite, and swelling at the site of the bite within a few minutes or up to 2 hours.

Breathing difficulty, paralysis, weakness, twitching, and numbness are also signs of neurotoxic venoms. These signs usually appear 1.5 to 2 hours after the bite.

Tip 70. Know your poisonous plants

To avoid potentially poisonous plants, stay away from any wild or unknown plants that have:

- Milky or discolored sap.
- Beans, bulbs, or seeds inside pods.
- Bitter or soapy taste.
- Spines, fine hairs, or thorns.
- Dill, carrot, parsnip, or parsleylike foliage.
- "Almond" scent in woody parts or leaves.
- Grain heads with pink, purplish, or black spurs.
- Three-leaved growth pattern.

Tip 71. Stay away from mushrooms

Mushroom identification is very difficult and must be precise, even more so than with other plants. Some mushrooms cause death very quickly. Some mushrooms have no known antidote. Two general types of mushroom poisoning are gastrointestinal and central nervous system. Symptoms of the most dangerous mushrooms affecting the central nervous system may show up after several days have passed when it is too late to reverse their effects.

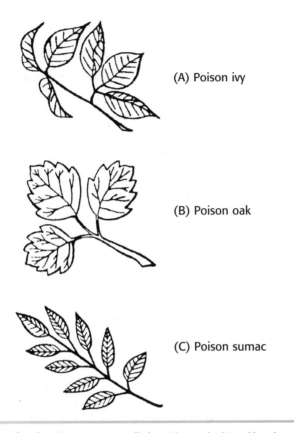

(A) Poison ivy

(B) Poison oak

(C) Poison sumac

Poison ivy (A) grows as a small plant (vine or shrub) and has three glossy leaflets. Poison oak (B) grows in shrub or vine form and has clusters of three leaflets with wavy edges. Poison sumac (C) grows as a shrub or small tree. Leaflets grow opposite each other with one at the tip.

Tip 72. React quickly to rashes

Common skin rashes can result from contact with various plants, such as poison ivy, poison oak, or poison sumac. Poison ivy grows as a small plant (vine or shrub) and has three glossy leaflets. Poison oak grows in shrub or vine form; and has clusters of three leaflets with wavy edges. Poison sumac grows as a shrub or small tree. Leaflets grow opposite each other with one at the tip. Symptoms are redness, swelling, itching, rashes or blisters, a burning sensation, and general headaches and fever. A secondary infection can occur when blisters break.

To treat these skin rashes, first expose the affected area and remove clothing and jewelry. Then cleanse the affected area with soap and water. Apply rubbing alcohol, if available, and then apply calamine lotion, which helps relieve itching and burning. Avoid dressing the affected area.

Chapter 7

Field-Expedient Direction Finding

In a survival situation, you will be extremely fortunate if you happen to have a map and compass. If you do have these two pieces of equipment, you will most likely be able to move toward help. If you are not proficient in using a map and compass, you must take the steps to gain these skills.

If you don't have a map or compass, there are several methods by which you can determine direction by using the sun, stars, and knowledge of the terrain. Once you have established your course, you may find that you have to cross a water obstacle. It may be in the form of a river, stream, lake, bog, quicksand, quagmire, or muskeg. Even in the desert, flash floods occur, making streams an obstacle. Whatever it is, you need to know how to make it safely across.

The compass-to-cheek method is used for sighting purposes only.

Tip 73. Sight with a compass

Fold the cover of the compass containing the sighting wire to a vertical position; then fold the rear sight slightly forward. Look through the rear-sight slot and align the front-sight hairline with the desired object in the distance. Then glance down at the dial through the eye lens to read the azimuth.

The compass-to-cheek technique is used almost exclusively for sighting, and it is the best technique for this purpose.

Tip 74. Make an improvised compass

You can construct improvised compasses using a piece of ferrous metal that can be needle shaped or a flat double-edged razor blade and a piece of nonmetallic string or long hair from which to suspend it. You can magnetize or polarize the metal by slowly stroking it in one direction on a piece of silk or carefully through your hair using deliberate strokes. You can also polarize metal by stroking it repeatedly at one end with a magnet. Always rub in one direction only. If you have a battery and some electric wire, you can polarize the metal electrically. The wire should be insulated. If not insulated, wrap the metal object in a single, thin strip of paper to prevent contact. The battery must be a minimum of 2 volts. Form a coil with the electric wire and touch its ends to the battery's terminals. Repeatedly insert one end of the metal object in and out of the coil. The needle will become an electromagnet. When suspended from a piece of non-metallic string, or floated on a small piece of wood in water, it will align itself with a north-south line.

Tip 75. Use a more elaborate compass

You can construct a more elaborate improvised compass using a sewing needle or thin metallic object, a nonmetallic container (for example, a plastic dip container), its lid with the center cut out and waterproofed, and the silver tip from a pen. To construct the compass, take an ordinary sewing needle and break it in half. One half will form your direction pointer and the other will act as the pivot point. Push the portion used as the pivot point through the bottom center of your container; this portion should be flush on the bottom and not interfere with the lid. Attach the center of the other portion (the pointer) of the needle on the pen's silver tip using glue, tree sap, or melted plastic. Magnetize one end of the pointer and rest it on the pivot point.

Tip 76. **Employ alternate means**

The old saying about using moss on a tree to indicate north is not accurate because moss grows completely around some trees. Actually, growth is more lush on the side of a tree facing the south in the Northern Hemisphere and vice versa in the Southern Hemisphere. If there are several felled trees around for comparison, look at the stumps. Growth is more vigorous in the side toward the equator and the tree growth rings will be more widely spaced. On the other hand, the tree growth rings will be closer together on the side toward the poles.

Wind direction may be helpful in some instances where there are prevailing directions and you know what they are.

Recognizing the difference between vegetation and moisture patterns on north- and south-facing slopes can aid in determining direction. In the Northern Hemisphere, north-facing slopes receive less sun than south-facing slopes and are therefore cooler and damper. In the summer, north-facing slopes retain patches of snow. In the winter, the trees and open areas on south-facing slopes are the first to lose their snow, and ground snowpack is shallower.

Tip 77. Use the sun and shadows

The earth's relationship to the sun can help you to determine direction on earth. The sun always rises in the east and sets in the west, but not exactly due east or due west. There is also some seasonal variation. In the Northern Hemisphere, the sun will be due south when at its highest point in the sky, or when an object casts no appreciable shadow. In the Southern Hemisphere, this same noonday sun will mark due north. In the Northern Hemisphere, shadows will move clockwise. Shadows will move counterclockwise to the Southern Hemisphere. With practice, you can use shadows to determine both direction and time of day. The shadow methods used for direction finding are the shadow-tip and watch methods.

1 Mark the shadow's tip.

2 Mark the new position
and draw a line through
the two marks.

3 Stand with the first mark to
your left and the second
mark to your right – you are
now facing north.

The shadow-tip method is a simple way of finding direction using the sun.

Tip 78. Learn shadow-tip methods

In the first shadow-tip method, find a straight stick 1 meter long, and a level spot free of brush on which the stick will cast a definite shadow. This method is simple and accurate and consists of four steps:

- Step 1. Place the stick or branch into the ground at a level spot where it will cast a distinctive shadow. Mark the shadow's tip with a stone, twig, or other means. This first shadow mark is always west—everywhere on earth.

- Step 2. Wait 10 to 15 minutes until the shadow tip moves a few centimeters. Mark the shadow tip's new position in the same way as the first.

- Step 3. Draw a straight line through the two marks to obtain an approximate east-west line.

- Step 4. Stand with the first mark (west) to your left and the second mark to your right—you are now facing the north. This fact is true everywhere on earth.

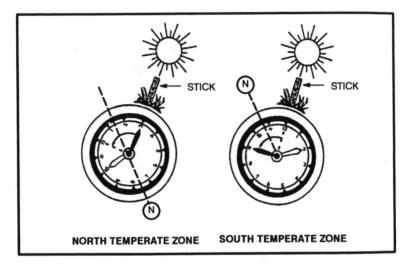

An analog watch can be used to determine the approximate true north and true south.

Tip 79. Find North with a watch

You can also determine direction using a common or analog watch. The direction will be accurate if you are using true local time, without any changes for daylight savings time. Remember, the further you are from the equator, the more accurate this method will be. If you only have a digital watch, you can overcome this obstacle. Quickly draw a watch on a circle of paper with the correct time on it and use it to determine your direction at that time.

In the Northern Hemisphere, hold the watch horizontal and point the hour hand at the sun. Bisect the angle between the hour hand and the 12 o'clock mark to get the north-south line. If there is any doubt as to which end of the line is north, remember that the sun rises in the east, sets in the west, and is due south at noon. The sun is in the east before noon and in the west after noon.

In the Southern Hemisphere, point the watch's 12 o'clock mark toward the sun and a midpoint halfway between 12 and the hour hand will give you the north-south line.

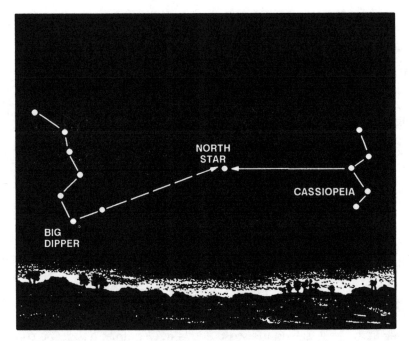

The Big Dipper and Cassiopeia, two constellations that never set, can be used to locate the North Star in the Northern Hemisphere.

Tip 80. Northern constellations

The main constellations in the Northern Hemisphere to learn are the Ursa Major, also known as the Big Dipper or the Plow, and Cassiopeia. Neither of these constellations ever sets. Use them to locate Polaris, also known as the polestar or the North Star. The Big Dipper and Cassiopeia are always directly opposite each other and rotate counterclockwise around Polaris, with Polaris in the center. The Big Dipper is a seven star constellation in the shape of a dipper. The two stars forming the outer lip of this dipper are the "pointer stars" because they point to the North Star. Mentally draw a line from the outer bottom star to the outer top star of the Big Dipper's bucket. Extend the line about five times the distance between the pointer stars. You will find the North Star along this distance.

After locating the North Star, find the North Pole or true north by drawing an imaginary line directly to the earth.

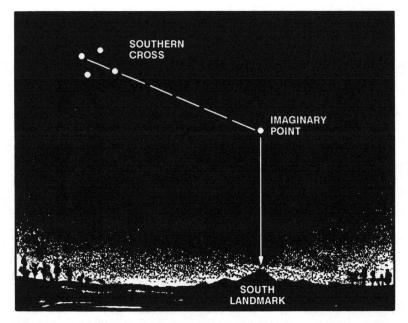

With its five stars, the Southern Cross is used as a signpost to the south in the Southern Hemisphere.

Tip 81. Southern constellations

Because there is no star bright enough to be easily recognized near the south celestial pole, a constellation known as the Southern Cross is used as a signpost to the south. The Southern Cross or Crux has five stars. Its four brightest stars form a cross that tilts to one side. The two stars that make up the cross's long axis are the pointer stars. To determine south, imagine a distance five times the distance between these stars and the point where this imaginary line ends is in the general direction of south. Look down to the horizon from the imaginary point and select a landmark to steer by. In the static survival situation, you can fix this location in daylight if you drive stakes in the ground at night to point the way.

Tip 82. Find direction by the moon

Because the moon has no light of its own, we can only see it when it reflects the sun's light. As it orbits the earth on its 28-day circuit, the shape of the reflected light varies according to its position. We say there is a new moon or no moon when it is on the opposite side of the earth from the sun. Then, as it moves away from the earth's shadow, it begins to reflect light from its right side and waxes to become a full moon before waning, or losing shape, to appear as a sliver on the left side. You can use this information to identify direction.

If the moon rises before the sun has set, the illuminated side will be the west. If the moon rises after midnight, the illuminated side will be the east. This obvious discovery provides us with a rough east-west reference during the night.

Tip 83. Avoid very cold water

When navigating in a survival situation, you must not try to swim or wade across a stream or river when the water is at very low temperatures. This swim could be fatal. Try to make a raft of some type. Wade across if you can get only your feet wet. Dry them vigorously as soon as you reach the other bank.

Tip 84. Locate a suitable crossing

You can apply almost any description to rivers and streams. They may be shallow or deep, slow or fast moving, narrow or wide. Before you try to cross a river or stream, develop a good plan.

Your first step is to look for a high place from which you can get a good view of the river or stream. From this place, you can look for a place to cross. If there is no high place, climb a tree. Good crossing locations include:

- A level stretch where it breaks into several channels. Two or three narrow channels are usually easier to cross than a wide river.
- A shallow bank or sandbar. If possible, select a point upstream from the bank or sandbar so that the current will carry you to it if you lose your footing.
- A course across the river that leads downstream so that you will cross the current at about a 45-degree angle.

Tip 85. Beware of dangerous obstacles

When crossing a river or stream, avoid the following potential hazards:

- Obstacles on the opposite side of the river that might hinder your travel. Try to select the spot from which travel will be the safest and easiest.

- A ledge of rocks that crosses the river. This often indicates dangerous rapids or canyons.

- Rocky places. You may sustain serious injuries from slipping or falling on rocks. Usually, submerged rocks are very slick, making balance extremely difficult. An occasional rock that breaks the current, however, may help you.

- An estuary of a river. An estuary is normally wide, has strong currents, and is subject to tides. These tides can influence some rivers many kilometers from their mouths. Go back upstream to an easier crossing site.

- Eddies. An eddy can produce a powerful backward pull downstream of the obstruction causing the eddy and pull you under the surface.

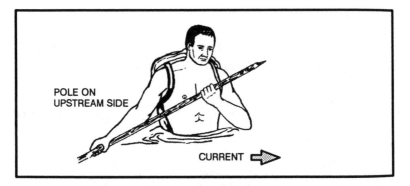

You can cross a swift stream with the help of a strong pole. It is also wise to carry your pack high on your shoulders so that is doesn't get soaked and become a burden.

Tip 86. Ford a treacherous stream

First, remove your pants and shirt to lessen the water's pull on you. Keep your footgear on to protect your feet and ankles from rocks. It will also provide you with firmer footing. Then tie your pants and other articles to the top of your rucksack or in a bundle, if you have no pack. This way, if you have to release your equipment, all your articles will be together. It is easier to find one large pack than to find several small items.

Carry your pack well up on your shoulders and be sure you can easily remove it, if necessary. Not being able to get a pack off quickly enough can drag even the strongest swimmers under. Find a strong pole to help you ford the stream. Plant it firmly on your upstream side to break the current. Plant your feet firmly with each step, and move the pole forward a little downstream from its previous position, but still upstream from you. With your next step, place your foot below the pole. Keep the pole well slanted so that the force of the current keeps the pole against your shoulder. Cross the stream at a 45-degree angle.

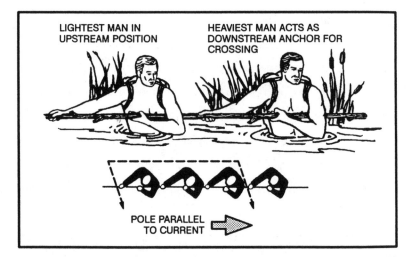

Several people can traverse a swift stream by using a formation designed to make sure everyone makes it across safely.

Tip 87. Cross a stream with a group

If you are with other people, cross a stream together. Ensure that everyone has his pack well up on his shoulders. Position the heaviest person on the downstream end of a long pole, and the lightest on the upstream end. In using this method, the upstream person breaks the current, and those below can move with relative ease in the eddy formed by the upstream person. If the upstream person gets temporarily swept off his feet, the others can hold steady while he regains his footing.

Tip 88. Swim with the rapids

If necessary, you can safely cross a deep, swift river or rapids. To swim across a deep, swift river, swim with the current, never fight it. Try to keep your body horizontal to the water. This will reduce the danger of being pulled under.

In fast, shallow rapids, lie on your back, feet pointing downstream, finning your hands alongside your hips. This action will increase buoyancy and help you steer away from obstacles. Keep your feet up to avoid getting them bruised or caught by rocks.

In deep rapids, lie on your stomach, head downstream, angling toward the shore whenever you can. Watch for obstacles and be careful of backwater eddies and converging currents, as they often contain dangerous swirls. Converging currents occur where new watercourses enter the river or where water has been diverted around large obstacles such as small islands.

Tip 89. Navigate through quicksand

Quicksand is a mixture of sand and water that forms a shifting mass. It yields easily to pressure and sucks down and engulfs objects resting on its surface. It varies in depth and is usually localized. Quicksand commonly occurs on flat shores, in silt-choked rivers with shifting watercourses, and near the mouths of large rivers. If you are uncertain whether a sandy area is quicksand, toss a small stone on it. The stone will sink in quicksand. Although quicksand has more suction than mud or muck, you can cross it just as you would cross a bog. Lie face down, spread your arms and legs, and move slowly across.

Chapter 8

Field-Expedient Weapons, Tools, and Equipment

In survival situations, you may have to

fashion any number and type of field-expedient tools and equipment to survive. Examples of tools and equipment that can make your life much easier are ropes, rucksacks, nets, and so on.

Weapons serve a dual purpose. You can use them to obtain and prepare food and to provide self-defense. A weapon can also give you a feeling of security and provide you with the ability to hunt on the move.

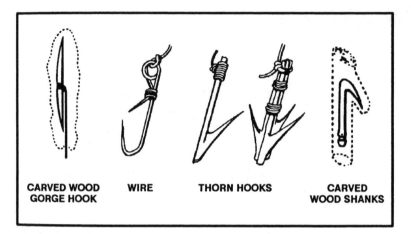

CARVED WOOD   **WIRE**   **THORN HOOKS**   **CARVED**
GORGE HOOK   **WOOD SHANKS**

From wood to wire, there are lots of materials to choose from when making improvised fishhooks.

Tip 90. Make your own fishhooks

You can make field-expedient fishhooks from pins, needles, wire, small nails, or any piece of metal. You can also use wood, bone, coconut shell, thorns, flint, seashell, or tortoise shell. You can also make fishhooks from any combination of these items.

To make a wooden hook, cut a piece of hardwood about 2.5 centimeters long and about 6 millimeters in diameter to form the shank. Cut a notch in one end in which to place the point. Place the point (piece of bone, wire, nail) in the notch. Hold the point in the notch and tie securely so that it does not move out of position. This is a fairly large hook. To make smaller hooks, use smaller material.

A gorge is a small shaft of wood, bone, metal, or other material. It is sharp on both ends and notched in the middle where you tie cordage. Bait the gorge by placing a piece of bait on it lengthwise. When the fish swallows the bait, it also swallows the gorge.

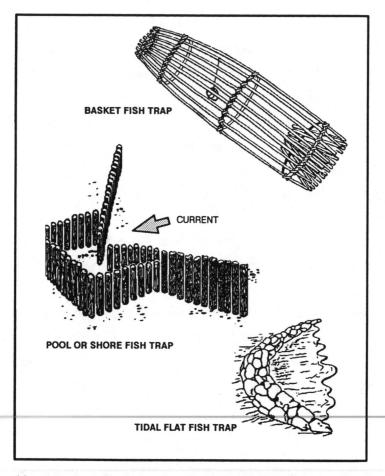

BASKET FISH TRAP

CURRENT

POOL OR SHORE FISH TRAP

TIDAL FLAT FISH TRAP

Fish traps can be made using a variety of methods, with the simplest involving the use of land features such as sandbars.

Tip 91. Build a fish trap

You may trap fish using several methods. Fish baskets are one method. You construct them by lashing several sticks together with vines into a funnel shape. You close the top, leaving a hole large enough for the fish to swim through. You can also use traps to catch saltwater fish, as schools regularly approach the shore with the incoming tide and often move parallel to the shore. Pick a location at high tide and build the trap at low tide. On rocky shores, use natural rock pools. On coral islands, use natural pools on the surface of reefs by blocking the openings as the tide recedes. On sandy shores, use sandbars and the ditches they enclose. Build the trap as a low stone wall extending outward into the water and forming an angle with the shore.

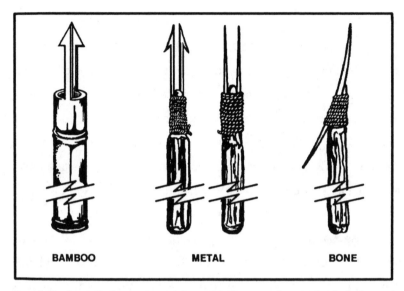

BAMBOO   **METAL**   **BONE**

Spearfishing is an effective way to catch larger fish. Use spears in water that is shallow and where the fish are most plentiful.

Tip 92. Catch fish with a spear

If you are near shallow water (about waist deep) where fish are large and plentiful, you can spear them. To make a spear, cut a long, straight sapling. Sharpen the end to a point or attach a knife, jagged piece of bone, or sharpened metal. You can also make a spear by splitting the shaft a few inches down from the end and inserting a piece of wood to act as a spreader. You then sharpen the two separated halves to points. To spear fish, find an area where fish either gather or where there is a fish run. Place the spear point into the water and slowly move it toward the fish. Then, with a sudden push, impale the fish on the stream bottom. Do not try to lift the fish with the spear, as it will probably slip off and you will lose it; hold the spear with one hand and grab and hold the fish with the other. Be alert to the problems caused by light refraction when looking at objects in the water.

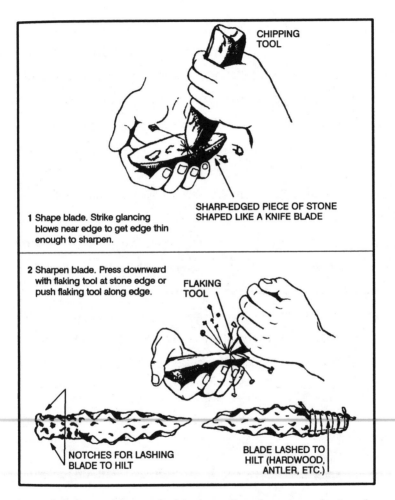

CHIPPING TOOL

SHARP-EDGED PIECE OF STONE SHAPED LIKE A KNIFE BLADE

1 Shape blade. Strike glancing blows near edge to get edge thin enough to sharpen.

2 Sharpen blade. Press downward with flaking tool at stone edge or push flaking tool along edge.

FLAKING TOOL

NOTCHES FOR LASHING BLADE TO HILT

BLADE LASHED TO HILT (HARDWOOD, ANTLER, ETC.)

A stone knife is one of the most basic and versatile tools you can make. It can be used as a weapon for hunting and as a cutting edge for food preparation.

Tip 93. Make a stone knife

To make a stone knife, you will need a sharp-edged piece of stone, a chipping tool, and a flaking tool. A chipping tool is a light, blunt-edged tool used to break off small pieces of stone. A flaking tool is a pointed tool used to break off thin, flattened pieces of stone. You can make a chipping tool from wood, bone, or metal, and a flaking tool from bone, antler tines, or soft iron.

Start making the knife by roughing out the desired shape on your sharp piece of stone, using the chipping tool. Try to make the knife fairly thin. Then, using the flaking tool, press it against the edges. This action will cause flakes to come off the opposite side of the edge, leaving a razor sharp edge. Use the flaking tool along the entire length of the edge you need to sharpen. Eventually, you will have a very sharp cutting edge that you can use as a knife.

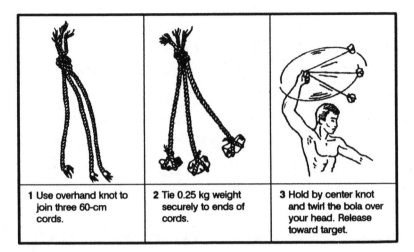

1 Use overhand knot to join three 60-cm cords.	**2** Tie 0.25 kg weight securely to ends of cords.	**3** Hold by center knot and twirl the bola over your head. Release toward target.

The bola is a primitive hunting tool that was used by various native peoples. It is extremely effective for capturing small game.

Tip 94. Make a bola

The bola is a field-expedient weapon that is easy to make. It is especially effective for capturing game or low-flying fowl in a flock. To use the bola, hold it by the center knot and twirl it above your head. Release the knot so that the bola flies toward your target. When you release the bola, the weighted cords will separate. These cords will wrap around and immobilize the fowl or animal that you hit.

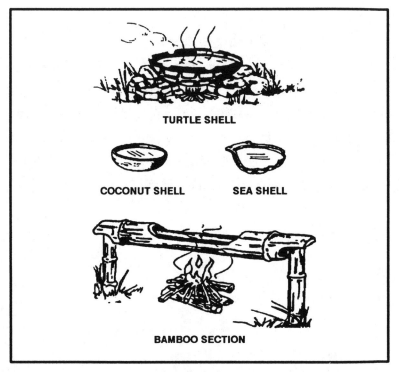

TURTLE SHELL

COCONUT SHELL   **SEA SHELL**

BAMBOO SECTION

With a little ingenuity, you will find that containers for boiling food can be made out of an assortment of natural materials.

Tip 95. Create makeshift cookware

Use wood, horn, bark, or other similar material to make bowls. To make wooden bowls, use a hollowed out piece of wood that will hold your food and enough water to cook it in. Hang the wooden container over the fire and add hot rocks to the water and food. Remove the rocks as they cool and add more hot rocks until your food is cooked. Do not use rocks with air pockets, such as limestone and sandstone. They may explode while heating in the fire.

You can also use this method with containers made of bark or leaves. However, these containers will burn above the waterline unless you keep them moist or keep the fire low. A section of bamboo works very well, if you cut out a section between two sealed joints. However, a sealed section of bamboo will explode if heated because of trapped air and water in the section.

Tip 96. Carve your own utensils

Carve forks, knives, and spoons from nonresinous woods so that you do not get a wood resin aftertaste or do not taint the food. Non-resinous woods include oak, birch, and other hardwood trees. Do not use trees that secrete a syrup or resinlike liquid on the bark or when cut.

Tip 97. Make a throwing stick

The throwing stick is very effective against small game. It is a blunt stick, naturally curved at about a 45-degree angle. Select a stick with the desired angle from a heavy hardwood such as oak. Shave off two opposite sides so that the stick is flat like a boomerang. You must practice the throwing technique for accuracy and speed. First, align the target by extending the nonthrowing arm in line with the mid to lower section of the target. Slowly and repeatedly raise the throwing arm up and back until the throwing stick crosses the back at about a 45-degree angle or is in line with the nonthrowing hip. Bring the throwing arm forward until it is just slightly above and parallel to the nonthrowing arm. This will be the throwing stick's release point. Practice slowly and repeatedly to attain accuracy.

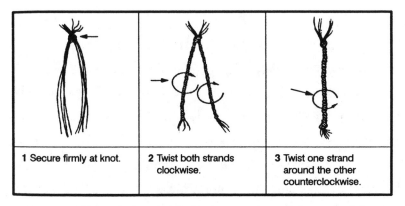

1 Secure firmly at knot.	2 Twist both strands clockwise.	3 Twist one strand around the other counterclockwise.

Lashing material is standard survival equipment. It can be made from animal sinew or plant fibers.

Tip 98. Braid lashing material

The best natural material for lashing small objects is sinew. You can make sinew from the tendons of large game, such as deer. Remove the tendons from the game and dry them completely. Smash the dried tendons so that they separate into fibers. Moisten the fibers and twist them into a continuous strand. If you need stronger lashing material, you can braid the strands. When you use sinew for small lashings, you do not need knots as the moistened sinew is sticky and it hardens when dry.

You can shred and braid plant fibers from the inner bark of some trees to make cord. You can use the linden, elm, hickory, white oak, mulberry, chestnut, and red and white cedar trees. After you make the cord, test it to be sure it is strong enough for your purpose. You can make these materials stronger by braiding several strands together.

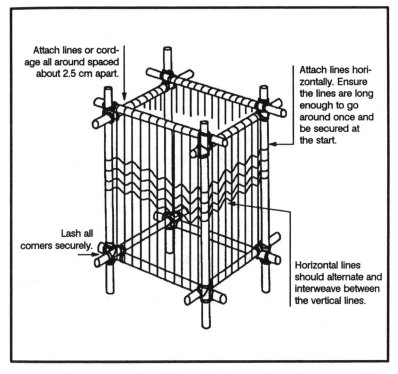

Attach lines or cord-
age all around spaced
about 2.5 cm apart.

Attach lines hori-
zontally. Ensure
the lines are long
enough to go
around once and
be secured at
the start.

Lash all
corners securely.

Horizontal lines
should alternate and
interweave between
the vertical lines.

A square pack is a simple and useful piece of equipment that can be constructed from whatever material is on hand.

Tip 99. Construct a square pack

The materials for constructing a pack are almost limitless. You can use wood, bamboo, rope, plant fiber, clothing, animal skins, and canvas.

This pack is easy to construct if rope or cordage is available. Otherwise, you must first make the cordage. To make this pack, construct a square frame from bamboo, limbs, or sticks. Size will vary for each person and the amount of equipment carried. (See figure on the opposite page.)

Tip 100. Select animal skins

The selection of animal skins in a survival situation will most often be limited to what you manage to trap or hunt. However, if there is an abundance of wildlife, select the hides of larger animals with heavier coats and large fat content. Do not use the skins of infected or diseased animals if at all possible. Since they live in the wild, animals are carriers of pests such as ticks, lice, and fleas. Because of these pests, use water to thoroughly clean any skin obtained from any animal. If water is not available, at least shake out the skin thoroughly. As with rawhide, lay out the skin, and remove all fat and meat. Dry the skin completely. Use the hind quarter joint areas to make shoes and mittens or socks. Wear the hide with the fur to the inside for its insulating factor.

Tip 101. Insulate with fibers

Several plants are sources of insulation from the cold. Cattail is a marshland plant found along lakes, ponds, and the backwaters of rivers. The fuzz on the tops of the stalks forms dead air spaces and makes a good downlike insulation when placed between two pieces of material. Milkweed has pollenlike seeds that act as good insulation. The husk fibers from coconuts are very good for weaving ropes and, when dried, make excellent tinder and insulation.